Team Up! 5

Gillian Baxter
Judith Rohlf

Cooperative-Learning Consultant: Jim Howden

STUDENT'S BOOK

ERPI ÉDITIONS DU RENOUVEAU PÉDAGOGIQUE INC.

5757, RUE CYPIHOT, SAINT-LAURENT (QUÉBEC) H4S 1R3
TÉLÉPHONE: (514) 334-2690 • TÉLÉCOPIEUR: (514) 334-4720
COURRIEL: erpidlm@erpi.com

Project editor: **Jeanine Floyd**

Cover and book design: **Tandem Conception et Infographie Inc.**

Illustrator: **Danielle Bélanger**

Songs: **Hjalmar Bardslokken**

Photo researcher: **Jaime Demperio**

Photographs:

The Gazette Photo Retail: cover; pp. 74, 75

Greebo Floyd-Jones: p. 46

Ron LeValley (Mad River Biologists): whales pp. 30, 32

Megapress Images: pp. 3; 21 b.r.; 28 t.r., b.l., b.m., b.r.; 28 row 1, row 3l., row 5, row 6; 29; 30; 32 t.; 46; 72 t.r., b.l., b.m., b.r.; 78; 79; 102 m.; 107 b.; 109; 110; 119 t.

Reflexion Phototheque: cover; pp. 21 t., b.l.; 28 row 2, row 3 r., row 4 both; 46; 72 t.l., t.m., m.; 99 m., b.; 102 t., b.; 107 t.; 119 b.

To Mario and Sarah, with love

Dépôt légal : 1er trimestre 1999
Bibliothèque nationale du Québec
National Library of Canada
Imprimé au Canada

ISBN 2-7613-0720-8

1234567890 ML 99
2190 ABCD   M12

Contents

Bienvenue en 5e année du primaire

As-tu déjà écouté une émission de télévision en anglais ? As-tu déjà lu une histoire en anglais ? Cela deviendra possible au fur et à mesure que ton apprentissage de l'anglais ne progresse.

Tu commences une nouvelle année du cours d'anglais et il est temps de continuer ta démarche d'apprentissage. Tout ce que tu as déjà appris peut t'aider et te donner confiance en ce début d'année scolaire.

Dans ton manuel *Team Up! 5*, tu trouveras beaucoup d'activités intéressantes et amusantes. Tu découvriras plusieurs domaines : animaux, sports, cultures, concours, etc. Ce manuel contient aussi quelques histoires courtes. Tu participeras à des projets excitants et plus encore.

Au cours de l'année, tu auras l'occasion de travailler seul et en équipe. Il est très important de participer à toutes les activités et de parler anglais. Tu peux toujours demander de l'aide à ton enseignant ou ton enseignante ainsi qu'aux camarades de classe. Ne crains pas de faire des erreurs. Personne ne se moquera de toi. Plus tu pratiqueras, meilleur tu seras.

Es-tu prêt ? Le temps est maintenant venu de commencer ta découverte de *Team Up! 5*. Joins-toi à l'équipe et amuse-toi.

Les auteures

Unit

1

WHAT'S IN A NAME?

James

Lady

Last but not least

Everybody has a name. You have a first name and a last name. Later on, you're going to make a name card. First, find out about different last names.

🔘 Listen to the information about last names.

🔘 Write down the answers as you listen.

To understand a factual description of a person, an animal, an event, an object or a place

2.2

JOHNSON, David

PAVELKO, Bogna

MARTINEZ, Pilar

CURRIE, Aaron

LEE, Shuang Guo

SINGH, Keero

ELAZHAR, Ahmed

CARTER, Sharon

LEDUC, Gabriel

What's in a name?

Most first names have a special meaning. Do you know what your name means? Find out about some first names.

🔊 Listen as some children tell you about their names.

🔊 Write down where their names come from and what they mean.

HELP STATION

► **Helpful expressions**

My name is . . .

It comes from . . .

My name was chosen because . . .

The meaning is . . .

The origin is . . .

It means . . .

This is my name because . . .

Decisions, decisions

On your name card you will explain what your name means and where it comes from. First, find out how these children got their names.

🔘 Read each child's story.

🔘 Find out the child's name, who chose it and why they chose it.

To understand someone who is describing a personal experience

1.6

We're Annie and Helene. Our mom named us for two very special people—our grandmothers. **1**

The children in my family are named for their godparents. I'm called Yvonne. I'm named for my godmother. **2**

My name is Bjorn. This is a Swedish name. My mom chose it because she liked it. **3**

I was born in China. My parents adopted me when I was six weeks old. They kept my Chinese name, Guo Shuang. My parents think it is a beautiful name. **4**

My dad's name is Saji. He was proud when I was born. He was happy to have a son. That's why he called me Saji—just like him. **5**

My big sister helped to choose my name. She chose Marila because it means "loved one". I know she loves me. **6**

I'm called Saburo because it means "third". I'm child number three in our family! **7**

My adoptive parents named me Theodore because it means "gift of God". I was like a special gift for them. They call me Theo. **8**

Tell me about your name.

You know what your name means and where it comes from. Now, find out about your teammate's name.

- Work with a partner.

- Ask your partner questions about his or her name.

- Answer your partner's questions about your name.

O.K., Hélène. Do you know what your name means?

Yeah. It means "sunshine". It's appropriate, no?

Oh yes! Where does this name come from?

It's of Greek origin.

Are you Greek?

No. I'm called Hélène because of my grandmother. She was Greek. It was her name.

That's neat!

 STATION

▶ **Helpful expressions**

What is your name?
How did you get your name?
Are you named for someone?

Please tell me about your name.
What does it mean?
What is the origin of your name?

5

Closure

Name card

Make a name card to put on your desk. Show everyone who you are!

- On the front of your card, write your name and illustrate it.
- On the back, write about your name.
- Tell your teammates about your name.

Polite
Active
Useful
Loving

My name is Paul.
This is my name because I am named for my grandfather.
The origin is Latin.
It means "small".
Paul

HELP STATION

▶ **Describing words**

calm *(calme)*	honest *(honnête)*	responsible *(digne de confiance)*
energetic *(actif)*	kind *(gentil)*	shy *(timide)*
generous *(généreux)*	patient *(patient)*	terrific *(formidable)*
happy *(heureux)*	polite *(poli)*	

Glossary

to choose

third

to choose: to take one thing over another *(choisir)*

family name: last name *(nom de famille)*

first name: given name *(prénom)*

godmother: woman who promises at a child's baptism to care for him or her *(marraine)*

to mean: to express or indicate *(vouloir dire)*

meaning: sense of a word *(sens)*

to name for: to give someone the name of another person *(donner à quelqu'un le nom de)*

origin: beginning *(origine)*

proud: to feel satisfied *(fier)*

third: last of three *(troisième)*

proud

More name facts . . .

1 Five popular names for dogs

1. Lady — 2. King   3. Duke

4. Pepe — 5. Prince

2 Five popular English names for girls and boys

1. Elizabeth 2. Louise 3. Alice 4. Charlotte 5. Mary	1. James 2. William 3. Alexander 4. Thomas 5. Edward

3 The longest English surname is Featherstonehaugh with 17 letters—can you beat that?

Guess who . . .

Match the person with the thing named for them.

1. Charles Rolls and Frederick Royce   2. Louis Braille   3. Earl of Sandwich
4. Samuel Morse   5. Lord Cardigan

a.   b.   c.   d.   e.

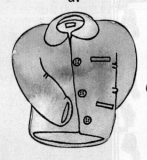 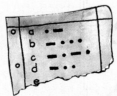   

Answers 1. D   2. E   3. B   4. C   5. A

Unit 2

FAMILY ALBUM

Who am I?

A family has many members—brothers, aunts, grandfathers and more. Find out about Sarah's family.

● Work with your team. Read about Sarah's family.

● Look at the pictures. Match all the people with their description.

● Write down the answers on your team answer sheet.

This is my family.

Most people like to talk about their families. Listen to some children introduce their family members to you.

- Listen to each child.

- Look at the pictures below.

- Match all the children with their family member.

To understand an introduction to another person or when a person says hello or goodbye

5.1

Yvonne

Taro

Karen

Haris

a.

b.

c.

d.

e.

f.

Family fun

Families like to do things together. Find out about family activities in different cultures.

● Listen to the children talk about their favourite family activity.

● Find out what each person likes to do.

● Put a check mark (✓) in the appropriate box on your handout.

My favourite family activity

What special activity does your family do together?

- Draw a picture of your favourite family activity.

- Write about this activity in your notebook.

To describe
yourself and
other people

1.4

A special person

Is there someone in your family who is very special to you? Read about Elizabeth's special person.

● Read about Elizabeth's uncle.

● Fill out your card with information about him.

A Special Person

My uncle is very special to me.
He's my mom's brother. He's 26 years old.
He has black hair. He wears glasses.

When I visit my uncle, I have fun.
He's very generous. He tells me stories.
He makes things for me. He made a desk
for my bedroom. He drives a red sports car.
It's really cool.

My uncle lives so far away. I wish I could
visit him more often. He's a special
person.

All about Graham

Graham is going to tell you about things that have happened to him and his family.

- Listen as Graham talks about himself.

- Fill in the missing information on Graham's time line.

- In your groups, read the information about Graham.

To understand a description of the major elements of a story: characters, conflict, events

To describe the major elements of a story: characters, conflict, events

3.2

My life

Remember Graham's time line? It's time for you to write about your life. What important things have happened to you and your family?

- Draw a time line.

- Write down the important events in your life.

- Share this information with your teammates.

Closure

Our family tree

1 You will understand and give information about your personal experiences and the experiences of people close to you.

5 You will understand and use the common expressions people use when they speak and write to each other.

You're going to make a class family tree.

- Help your classmates to prepare the tree.

- Write all about your family on your leaf.

- Glue your leaf on the class family tree.

Glossary

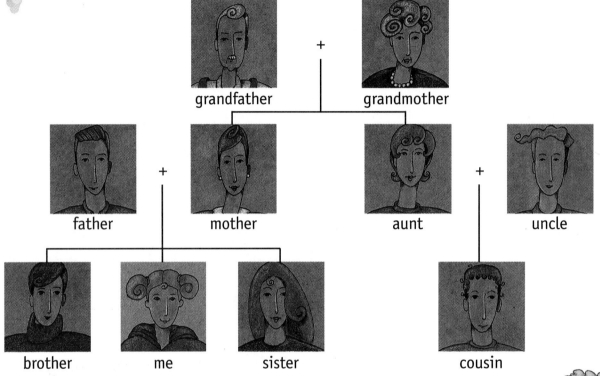

grandfather + grandmother

father + mother / aunt + uncle

brother / me / sister / cousin

computer whiz: person who knows a lot about computers *(amateur de l'informatique)*

curly: twisted, like waves *(bouclé)*

family tree: plan showing someone's family *(arbre généalogique)*

far away: at a distance *(loin)*

glasses: object worn to help poor eyesight *(lunettes)*

leather: animal skin used to make shoes and clothes *(cuir)*

short: not long *(court)*

stepmother: woman who marries a person's father (not the person's birth mother) *(belle-mère)*

straight: not wavy or twisted *(raide)*

time line: line showing important dates in a person's life *(ligne du temps)*

twins: two children born at the same time of the same mother *(jumeaux)*

curly

glasses

twins

Unit

3

Our team

Who are you?

During this unit, you are going to work with your new team. Who are your new teammates? Who will you work with? Get to know someone on your team.

 Work with a partner.

 Tell your partner who you are. Tell him or her one fact about yourself.

 Find out about your partner.

To understand who someone is

To say who you are

1.1

Our team

Now you know one person in your team. What about the others?

ACTIVITY

🔊 Introduce your partner to your team.

🔊 Listen to your other teammates and find out about them.

To understand an introduction to another person or when a person says hello or goodbye

5.1

> This is my teammate, Graham. He likes to play soccer.

> This is Stella. She comes from Greece.

> I'd like to introduce my partner, Stephen. He plays the trumpet.

> This is Brigitte. She's 10 years old.

All about Keero

Soon you will make an identity card for yourself. Practise by making one for Keero.

Listen to the description of Keero.

Fill in the information on his identity card.

To understand
a factual
description
of a person,
an animal,
an event,
an object or
a place

2.2

What are your roles?

Everyone in the team has an important job. Each person is responsible for his or her own role. Learn about some of the roles you will have.

🔊 Listen as Vanessa, Aaron, Keero and Pilar describe what they will do.

🔊 Identify each person's job.

🔊 Write down the answers.

Team tips

A good team needs some rules to follow. Find out what you must do to be a good team. Think about the rules you will write in your team passport.

○ Read "Team Tips".

○ Write down the team tips in your notebook.

○ Share your answers and complete your team handout.

Team tips

Here's how to make sure your team is a success:

- Your team must work together. You must help each other. Your team must share materials and share the work.

- Each person is important. You must all participate. You must all share your ideas. You must have a role and do your job.

- You must try to speak English. It is important to practise.

Try it! You can have a winning team.

Our experiences

Each person in the team has something important to do. What can you do to be a good teammate?

🔊 Listen to the four students talk about their experiences on their team.

🔊 Write down what each person did.

🔊 Work with your teammates. Complete your team answer sheet.

To understand someone who is describing a personal experience

1.6

ROLES

Materials Manager	You pick up and return materials for your team.
Recorder	You write down your team's answers.
Speaker	You report your team's answers.
Captain Quiet	You make sure your teammates speak quietly.

25

Closure
Team passport

1 You will understand and give information about your personal experiences and the experiences of people close to you.

2 You will understand and give information about things outside your everyday life.

4 You will understand and give information about activities related primarily to school life.

Now you're ready to make your team passport.

- ◉ Complete your identity card.

- ◉ Read the information to your teammates.

- ◉ Find a name and a symbol for your team.

- ◉ Write your team contract.

- ◉ Glue everything on construction paper.

Now you have your team passport! Tell the class about your team.

The Bookworms

NAME: Keero
AGE: ten
BIRTHDAY: June 5th
HAIR: black
EYES: brown
FAVOURITE SPORT: soccer
FAVOURITE COLOUR: red
HOBBIES: drawing, reading, watching TV
QUALITIES: generous, patient
PROMISE: I will listen to my teammates' ideas
Keero Singh

THE BOOKWORMS' CONTRACT

We will speak in English.
We have to help each other.
We must work together.
We're going to listen to each other.

Keero   Pilar
Garon   Vanessa

Glossary

to listen

quiet

to glue

to disturb: to break the quiet or calm *(déranger)*

to glue: to stick *(coller)*

to help: to give service *(aider)*

hobby: activity you do for fun *(passe-temps)*

to listen: to give attention to *(écouter)*

to perform: to do something *(exécuter)*

quality: good character trait *(qualité)*

rules: regulations *(règlements)*

quiet: silent; calm *(silencieux; tranquille)*

to share: to divide into parts; participate *(partager; participer)*

shy: timid *(timide)*

tip: useful piece of information *(renseignement)*

together: as a group *(ensemble)*

to try: to make an effort *(essayer)*

winning team: best group
(équipe gagnante)

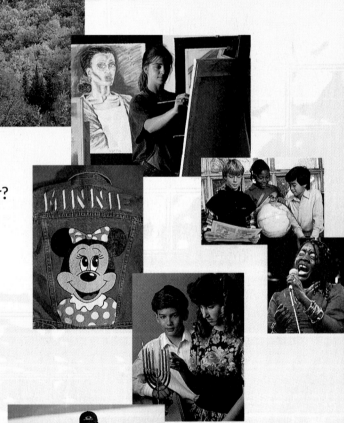

You can still learn more about your teammates. Why not do a team interview?
Find out your teammates' favourite things. Here's how:

- Each person takes a turn to be interviewed.
- The other team members interview that person.
- After two minutes, the person sits down and the next person is interviewed.

Here are some questions to ask.

1. What is your favourite season?

2. What is your favourite TV show?

3. What is your favourite pastime?

4. What is your favourite kind of movie?

5. Who is your favourite cartoon character?

6. What is your favourite school subject?

7. What is your favourite holiday?

8. Who is your favourite singer?

9. What is your favourite winter activity?

10. What is your favourite animal?

Unit 4

QUÉBEC WILDLIFE

To say what
you like, dislike,
want or prefer

1.2

The animal kingdom

Do you like animals? Which ones? Are there any animals that you do not like?

- Look at the poster of the animals.

- Write down the animals you like. Then write down the animals you dislike.

Our favourite animals

On your team poster you will describe a wild animal that lives in Québec. Which wild animal is your favourite? What colour is it? What does it eat? How big is it?

- Write down information about your animal on the wildlife identification card.

- Share your information with the other members of your team.

- Decide which animal you will describe on your team poster.

MY FAVOURITE ANIMAL
Animal: red fox
Colour: red
Size: small, thin
Habitat: fields, forests
Food: meat, insects, berries
Trait: can run fast

To give a factual description of a person, an animal, an event, an object or a place

2.2

31

To understand the major elements of a story: characters, conflict, events

A. Wildlife wonders

There are many wildlife parks in Québec. You can learn about different animals there. Read a brochure about Québec wildlife.

- Read the brochure.
- Name the animals on the handout.
- Match each animal with its habitat.
- What is the habitat of the animal you will describe on your team poster?

WILDLIFE WONDERS

WILDLIFE

Animals need certain conditions to survive. They need food, shelter and space. This is called their habitat.

Forest

In Québec, some animals live in the forest. There are foxes. You can also find deer. There might even be a black bear.

Gulf of St Lawrence

Here there are whales. You can see beluga and blue whales. There are even some seals.

Northern Québec

Travel north to find special wildlife. Here it is very cold. Polar bears and caribou live in this region.

Every area of Québec has its own wildlife. Visit these places to see some special animals.

B. Can you find me?

At some nature reserves, guides explain where certain animals are found.
Find out where each animal lives.

🔘 Listen as the guide gives directions around Québec.

🔘 Trace the routes on your map.

🔘 Write the name of the animal that lives in each region.

ACTIVITY

To understand
how to get to a
certain place

4.3

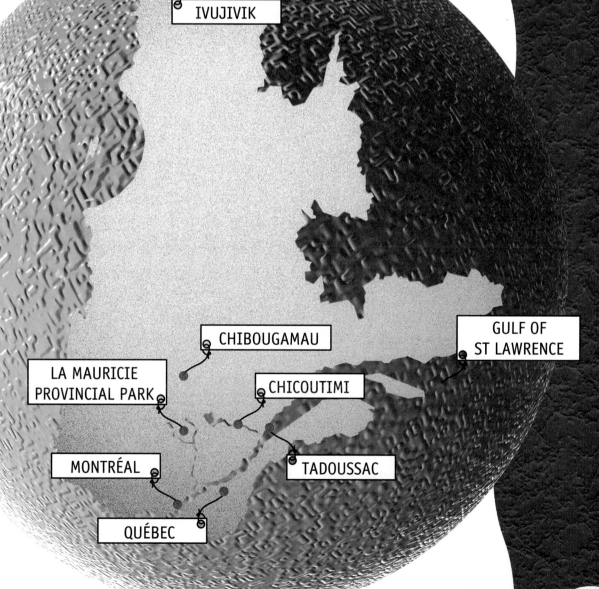

IVUJIVIK

CHIBOUGAMAU

GULF OF
ST LAWRENCE

LA MAURICIE
PROVINCIAL PARK

CHICOUTIMI

MONTRÉAL

TADOUSSAC

QUÉBEC

Be careful!

Before you go outdoors, you should know some safety rules. You will include a warning on your wildlife poster.

⬤ Look at the situations on your handout.

⬤ Listen to the safety tips.

⬤ Are the children following the rules? Write down the numbers of the pictures where they are not obeying a rule.

Bear facts

The guide from the nature reserve is talking on a radio show. She talks about polar bears and black bears. You can use this information for your team poster.

- Listen to the guide.

- Complete your information card while you listen.

- Work with your team. Write down how polar bears and black bears are similar and how they are different.

Closure
Team wildlife poster

1 You will understand and give information about your personal experiences and the experiences of people close to you.

2 You will understand and give information about things outside your everyday life.

4 You will understand and give information about activities related primarily to school life.

What do you remember about wild animals in Québec? It's time for you to create a team poster about Québec wildlife.

⚫ Do you remember which animal you chose in Activity 2? On the map of Québec, show where this animal lives.

⚫ Draw a picture of your animal.

⚫ Combine your information to make your team poster.

Glossary

berry: kind of small, round, juicy fruit, like a blueberry or raspberry *(baie)*

both: two *(les deux)*

careful: cautious *(prudent)*

to climb: to go up *(monter)*

habitat: natural home of animals *(habitat)*

map: plan of a place *(carte)*

near: close *(près de)*

shelter: protection against weather or enemies *(abri)*

size: how big or small something is *(taille)*

trait: characteristic *(trait)*

wildlife: wild animals *(animaux sauvages)*

to climb

shelter

map

wild animal

Do you know . . .?

What's the fastest animal? How many hours does a lion sleep?

- Work with your team.

- Look at the pictures.

- Play the Mystery Animal game.

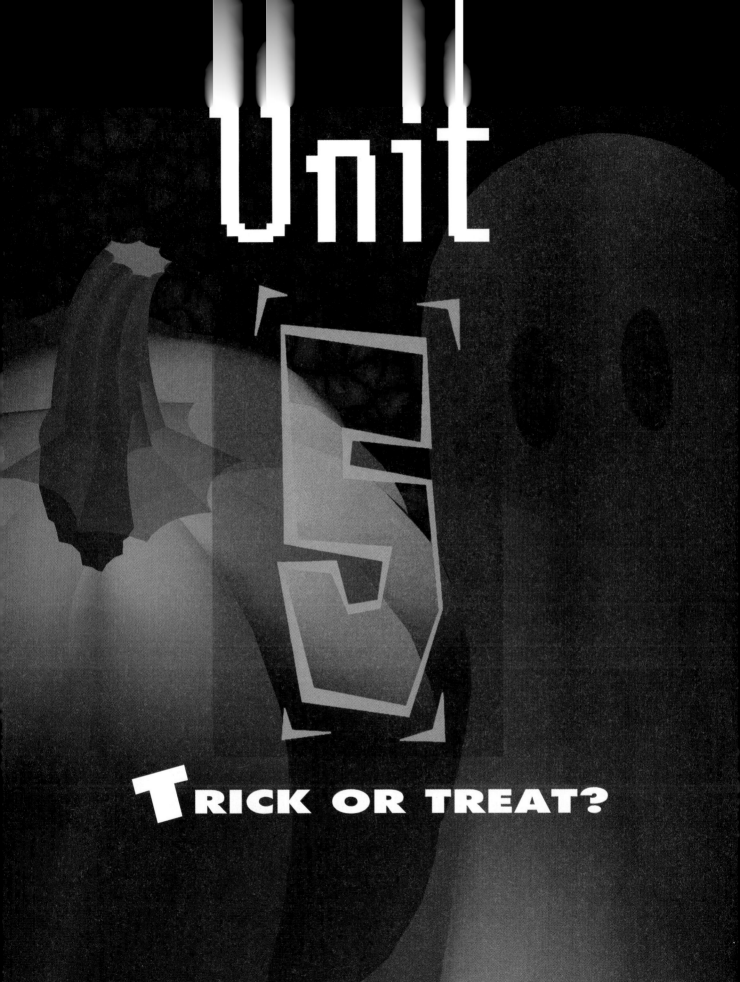

Unit 5

TRICK OR TREAT?

It's Halloween!

It's Halloween! Here's a Halloween crossword.

● Read the clues on your clue card. Find the answers in the Halloween picture.

● Work with your team. Fill in the crossword puzzle with the Halloween words.

Halloween words

To understand a factual description of a person, an animal, an event, an object or a place

2.2

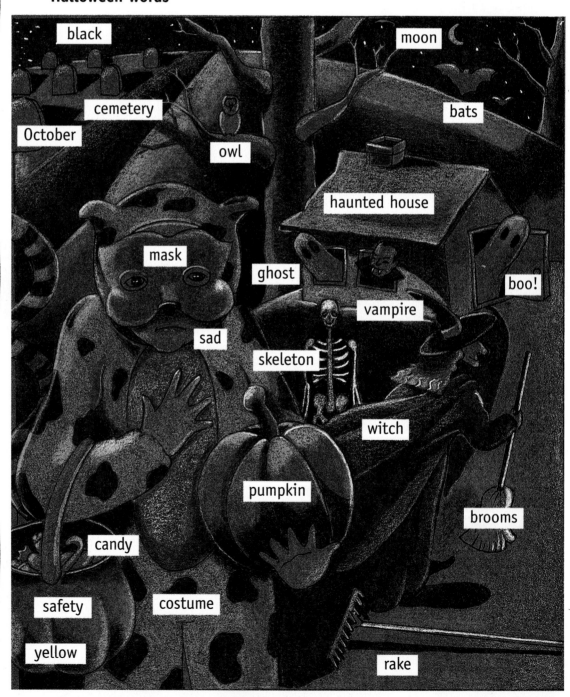

black
moon
cemetery
bats
October
owl
haunted house
mask
ghost
boo!
vampire
sad
skeleton
witch
pumpkin
brooms
candy
safety
costume
yellow
rake

What should I wear?

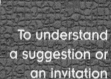

It's fun to wear an original costume at Halloween. Listen to some students' ideas.

● Listen to the students' conversation.

● Write down the letters of the costumes the students suggest.

● Draw a picture of the costume that Linda will wear.

To understand
a suggestion or
an invitation

4.6

41

Play it safe!

Halloween is a time to have fun but it is also important to be safe.

⬤ Read "Halloween Safety".

⬤ Work with your team. Read the statements your teacher gives you.

⬤ Decide whether the statements represent good ideas or bad ideas.

To understand
a warning or
caution

4.5

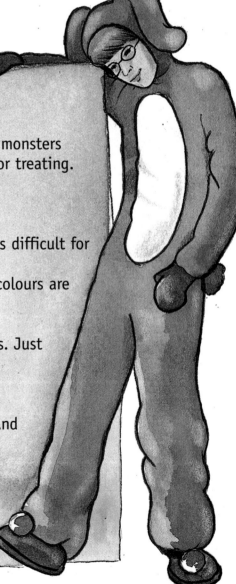

Halloween Safety

On October 31, you're sure to see ghosts, clowns, monsters
and witches! It's Halloween! It's time to go trick or treating.

To have a safe Halloween, follow these rules.

1. Costumes are great but don't wear a mask. It's difficult for
   you to see.
2. Wear light colours like white or yellow. Dark colours are
   not visible.
3. Don't go out alone. Stay in a group.
4. It's not a good idea to go into strange houses. Just
   stay outside.
5. Watch out for cars when you cross the street.
   Between houses, stay on the sidewalk.
6. Finally, before you eat your candy, check it. And
   don't eat it all at once!

Halloween is great fun! Have a super time and
play it safe!

What should you do?

You know how to have a safe Halloween. Can you tell other students what they should or should not do?

- Look at the picture.

- Find five problems in the picture.

- Give a warning for each problem.

Making faces

ACTIVITY

To understand instructions

4.1

To understand polite forms for saying thank you, sorry.

5.2

Pumpkins are very popular at Halloween. You can carve different faces on them and dress them up.

Listen to the instructions for each of the pumpkins.

Follow the instructions and colour in the pumpkins on your handout.

Happy Halloween

How can you be sure to have a good and safe Halloween? What must you do?

- Work with your team. Decide on four rules to have a happy Halloween.

- Take turns writing the rules.

To say what you or someone else must do

4.4

Closure
Trick or treat?

2 You will understand and give information about things outside your everyday life.

4 You will understand and give information about activities related primarily to school life.

You have learned many new Halloween words. Use them to play Halloween bingo.

- Look at the word cards with your teammates.

- Turn over five cards.

- Listen to your teacher's definition of different words. If you have that word, flip the card over.

- When four of your cards are flipped over, call out "Trick or treat?"

Good luck!

Glossary

alone: apart from other people *(tout seul)*

bone: hard substance that forms the skeleton *(os)*

to carve: to cut *(sculpter)*

cookie sheet: metal tray used for baking cookies *(tôle à biscuit)*

to empty: to take out the contents *(vider)*

garbage: rubbish *(ordures)*

hole: opening *(trou)*

lollipop: piece of hard candy on the end of a stick *(suçon)*

recipe: directions for preparing something to eat *(recette)*

rule: regulation *(règlement)*

to spread: to cover *(étendre)*

to sprinkle: to cover with small pieces *(saupoudrer)*

turnip: round orange vegetable *(navet)*

From pumpkin to jack-o'-lantern

1. Choose a pumpkin.

Wow! Look at this big one!

2. Use a marker and draw a face on the pumpkin.

Let's give it a happy face.

3. Cut off the top of the pumpkin. Ask an adult to help you.

4. Empty the pumpkin.

Let's save the seeds and toast them.

5. Get help to carve the eyes, nose and mouth.

There we go!

6. Put a candle inside.

Ahhhh!

Did you know . . .

. . . jack-o'-lanterns were used to chase away evil spirits?

. . . there were no pumpkins in Ireland, so children used potatoes and turnips?

. . . the biggest pumpkin was grown in Washington and weighed 376 kilograms?

. . . a pumpkinseed is a kind of fish?

. . . you can toast pumpkin seeds? They're delicious. Here's the recipe—ask an adult to help you make them.

Toasted pumpkin seeds

1. Rinse the seeds and let them dry.

2. Pour two tablespoons of vegetable oil over the seeds.

3. Sprinkle the seeds with salt.

4. Spread the seeds on a cookie sheet.

5. Bake for 15 minutes at 180°C.

Unit

THE VANISHING VISITORS

The vanishing visitors

Two brothers have a strange experience with some very strange creatures. Find out what happens.

🔊 Read the summary. Then listen to the story.

🔊 Complete the puzzle. Find the name of the visitors' home planet.

The summary

R.J. and T.J. are at home alone. Suddenly, the electricity goes out. Everything is black. The boys see yellow, purple and green lights. The twins are scared. They look out of the window and see —. What do they see? Who is in their backyard? Listen to the story and find out.

What happened?

Did you really understand the story? Do this activity just to make sure.

🔊 Work with your team. Take turns reading the sentences.

🔊 Match the pictures with the sentences.

1. Two brothers are alone at home.

2. Everything goes black. There are flashing lights outside.

3. The boys look out of the window.

4. The boys see a space ship and five strange people.

5. One of the boys takes some pictures of the space ship.

6. The doorbell rings. The boys are scared. They hide in the closet.

7. Their mother returns and everything is normal.

8. The film is developed but there are no pictures of the visitors.

How are you feeling?

How did R.J. and T.J. feel when they saw the space ship? How do you think the space people felt?

- Read the conversations.

- Which faces show how the people feel? Write down the numbers.

A visitor vanishes!

One of the space people didn't leave on the space ship. She was left behind!

⦿ Look at the creatures below.

⦿ Listen to the description of the visitor.

⦿ Identify which visitor was left behind.

⦿ Work with your team. Take turns describing the other space people.

To understand
who someone is

1.1

To give a factual
description of
a person,
an animal,
an event,
an object or
a place

2.2

55

What do they look like?

Use your imagination to create a space person. Follow these instructions.

- Work with your team. Write down the four characteristics of the visitors in the story.

- Add new characteristics—two per person. Be original.

- Draw a picture of your creature with your teammates.

- Give your creature a name.

- Write a short description of your creature.

To give a factual description of a person, an animal, an event, an object or a place

2.2

Can you believe it? They have only two arms!

Look where their noses are! That's strange!

Look! Their legs bend at the knees!

Closure

Hey, wait for me!

Play a game about the story. Be the first in your group to help V.G.-6 back to her space ship before it returns home. Have fun! Good luck!

- Read the rules.

- Play the game with your teammates.

The rules

1. Roll the die. The person with the highest number begins.

2. Move around the board clockwise.

3. More than one player can occupy a square at the same time.

4. You must have the exact number to win.

HELP STATION

► **Some useful expressions**

It's your turn / my turn.
Hurry up!
Correct!

Lose a turn.
Too bad!
Next!

ZORBO HERE WE COME!

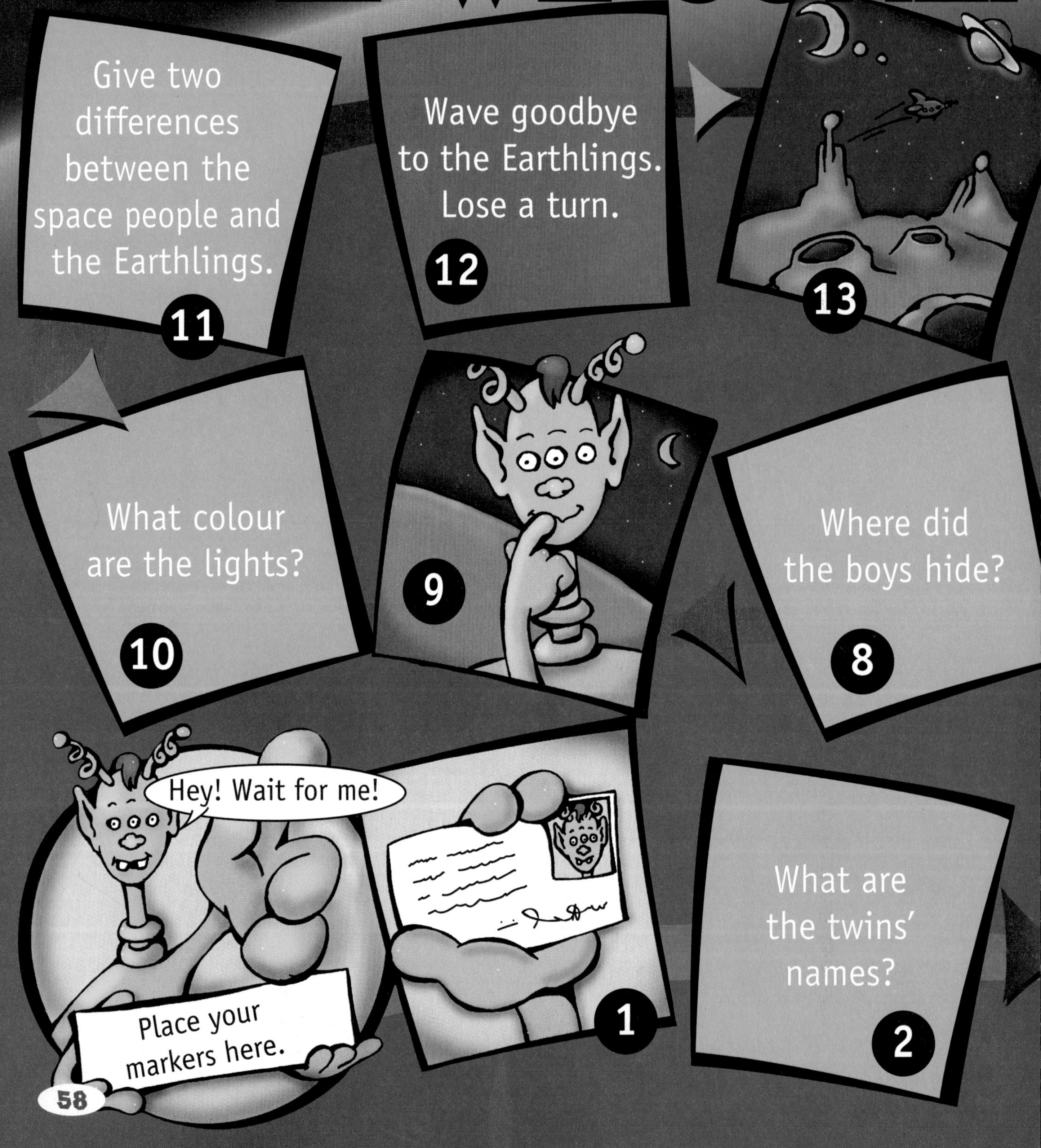

You're almost there! Are you sure you want to leave Earth? Take your next turn to think about it. **14**

15

So long, Earthlings!

Hurry up. We're leaving!

Zorbo, here we come!

Hey! We can't leave without V.G.-6!

Name two characteristics of the space people. **7**

You're in a hurry. Play again. **6**

How many eyes do the space people have? **5**

How many space people did the twins see? **3**

4

Glossary

backyard: small piece of land behind a house *(cour)*
closet: cupboard for hanging clothes *(armoire)*
pointed: having a sharp end *(pointu)*
scared: frightened *(effrayé)*
space ship: vehicle designed to fly in space *(vaisseau, véhicule spatial)*

small: *(petit)*   **big:** *(gros)*   **long:** *(long)*   **short:** *(court)*

small   big   long   short

Parts of the body

antenna
hair
forehead
head
arm
elbow
hand
finger
hip

eye
ear
nose
mouth
chin
neck
body

Hello! I'm X.Y.-17.
You Earthlings sure look
strange.

leg
knee
ankle
foot
toe

Unit

7

To you from me

I care!

Tommy has something for his sister. Can you guess what it is?

- Read the comic strip.

- Play the story spinner game with your teammates.

To understand a description of the major elements of a story: characters, conflict, events

To describe the major elements of a story: characters, conflict, events

3.2

Special days

There are many times during the year when you can send a greeting card to your family or friends.

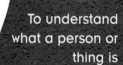

◉ Listen to the description of some special events.

◉ Write the events on the calendar.

To understand what a person or thing is

2.1

A celebration of life

Find out about a new celebration. Kwanzaa is a special time for Afro-American people.

 Listen to the description of Kwanzaa.

 Answer the questions *who? what? when?* and *how?*

What's the occasion?

Greeting cards usually have a special message inside. There's a message for every occasion.

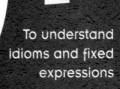

To understand idioms and fixed expressions

5.4

- Look at the cards.

- Listen to the people talking.

- Decide which message is the best for each card.

Happy or sad?

As you know, there are many reasons for sending a greeting card. You can send a card to say "thanks" or a card to say "sorry".

⬤ Read the messages below.

⬤ Draw a happy face 🙂 for the thank-you messages

and a sad face 🙁 for the sorry messages.

1. I forgot your birthday. Please excuse me.

2. Your kindness is greatly appreciated

3. I am very grateful for your help.

4. I hurt you. I regret it. Please forgive me.

5. To thoughtful you from thankful me.

Message match

As you've learned, greeting cards can contain different messages.

🔘 Look at the pictures.

🔘 Give an appropriate message for each one.

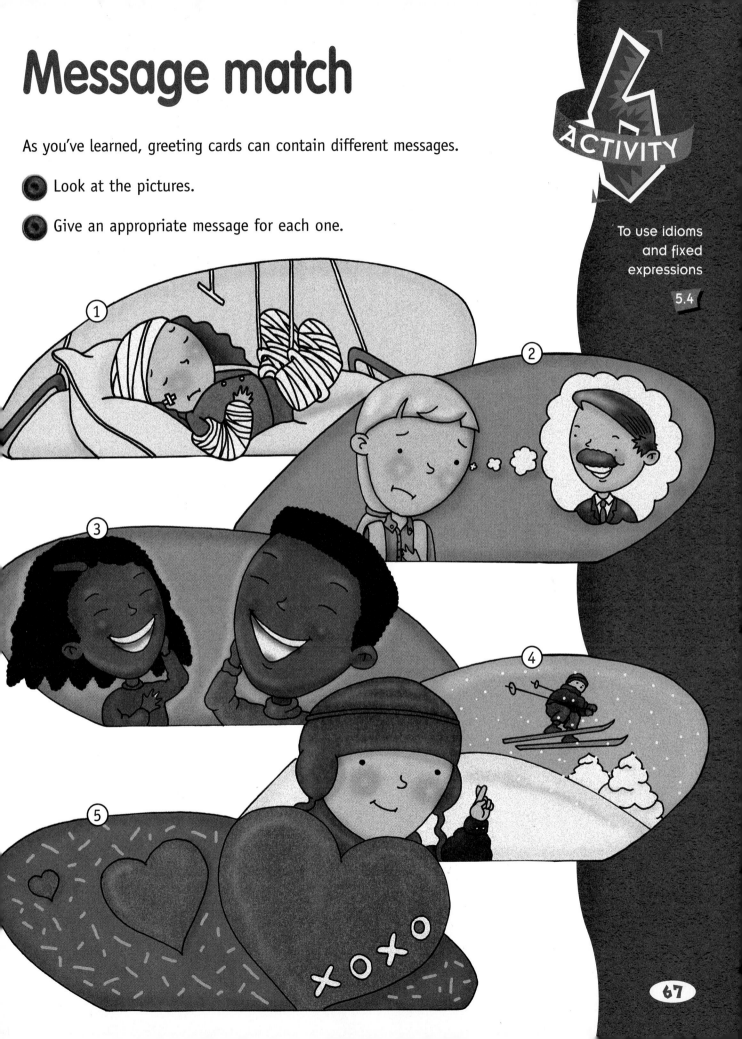

To understand
instructions

4.1

A pop-up greeting

Do you know how to make a pop-up greeting card?

⚫ Look at the pictures.

⚫ Read the instructions.

⚫ Work with your team. Match each instruction with an illustration.

1. Take a piece of paper and fold it in half. Then, fold it in half again.
2. Open the paper so it is folded only one time.
3. Fold the top left corner down to the centre line. Fold the bottom left corner to the centre line.
4. Open the paper so it is folded in half.
5. Draw two curved lines. Cut the lines.
6. Open the paper like a tent.
7. Push the curves inside. Your card looks like a moustache.
8. Open the card. Draw some petals and add leaves.
9. Glue the card to a second piece of paper. Don't glue the pop-up petals!

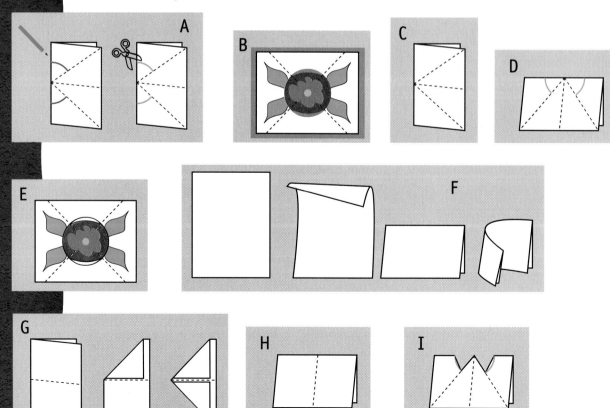

Closure
To you from me

Why not make a greeting card for someone special?

Follow the instructions in Activity 7 to make a pop-up card.

Then follow these steps.

1. Choose a message for your card.
2. Write part of the message on the outside.
3. Write the rest of the message inside.
4. Decorate your card.
5. Choose a person to give the card to.
6. Sign the card with your name.
7. If you want, make an envelope for your card.
8. Address the envelope.
9. Show your card to your teammates.
10. Give or send your card to that special person.

2 — You will understand and give information about things outside your everyday life.

4 — You will understand and give information about activities related primarily to school life.

5 — You will understand and use the common expressions people use when they speak and write to each other.

Glossary

to care: to be concerned *(se soucier de)*

to cheer up: to make more cheerful *(relever le moral)*

to exchange: to give in return for something *(échanger)*

expensive: costing a lot of money *(cher)*

to forgive: to pardon *(pardonner)*

gift: something given to someone as a present *(cadeau)*

grateful: feeling thankful *(reconnaissant)*

greeting card: illustrated card with a short message *(carte de souhaits)*

happy: joyful *(heureux)*

to hurt: to injure *(blesser)*

to last: to take a certain time *(durer)*

to laugh: to show amusement *(rire)*

relative: family *(famille)*

to take place: to happen *(avoir lieu)*

thankful: feeling grateful *(reconnaissant)*

thoughtful: concerned *(gentil)*

sad: unhappy *(triste)*

sick: ill *(malade)*

to wish: to want *(souhaiter)*

happy

sad

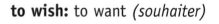

relative

Unit

8

SPORTSMANIA

What do you think?

Who is your favourite athlete? What is your favourite sport? What do you think about the world of sports?

◉ Tell your classmates what you think about sports.

◉ In your sports booklet, write down your favourite sport.

HELP STATION

► **Giving opinions**

I think . . . / I don't think . . .   I believe . . .   I feel that . . .

Our talents

People have different talents and abilities. Some are good musicians or artists. Others are good athletes. Everybody can do something special.

🔊 Listen to the interview on Sportsmania.

🔊 Match the athletes with their sports.

🔊 Choose the pictures that show what the athletes do especially well.

🔊 In your sports booklet, write down something that you are good at.

To understand what someone can or cannot do

1.3

To understand someone who asks for information or for an explanation

5.3

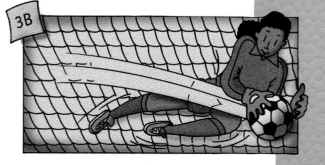

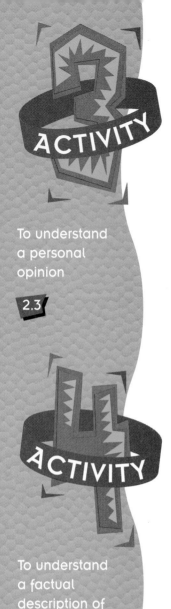

ACTIVITY

Making it work

Being a good athlete is not easy, especially when you play on a team. Sportsmania interviewed Mario. He plays volleyball.

 Listen to the interview with Mario.

 In your sports booklet, write down three things that you need to do to be a good athlete and teammate.

To understand a personal opinion

2.3

ACTIVITY

The Stanley Cup

An important sports event is the Stanley Cup playoffs. Here is a special report from Sportsmania.

 Listen to the Sportsmania radio report.

 On your team handout, write down the information about the Stanley Cup.

 In your sports booklet, write down your favourite hockey team or player.

To understand a factual description of a person, an animal, an event, an object or a place

2.3

The Olympic games

The most important international sports event is the Olympic games.

 Listen to the story of the Olympic games.

 Work with your team. Write a summary of the Olympics. (Look at the pictures if you need help.)

 In your sports booklet, write down two Olympic sports.

ATLANTA

75

Closure

The wide world of sports

Do you play a sport? Who is your favourite athlete? Which team do you like? Prepare a sports presentation for your teammates.

- Choose your subject.

- In your sports booklet, write a short text about your subject.

- Add some pictures for your presentation.

- Present your information to your teammates.

1 You will understand and give information about your personal experiences and the experiences of people close to you.

2 You will understand and give information about things outside your everyday life.

Glossary

engraved: cut in *(gravé)*
event: important happening *(événement)*
goalie: player who guards the goal *(gardien de but)*
height: how tall something is *(hauteur)*
high: tall *(haut)*
home run: in baseball, running around all the bases to score a point *(coup de circuit)*
laurel wreath: crown of leaves *(couronne de lauriers)*
net: open material made of cord *(filet)*
playoffs: game played to determine the winners of a championship *(match de barrage)*
race: competition to see who is the fastest *(course)*
ring: circle *(anneau)*
silver: metal *(argent)*
width: how wide something is *(largeur)*
winner: victor *(gagnant)*

height

laurel wreath

silver

net

goalie

Olympic facts

Did you know . . .

. . . that the 1976 Olympic games were held in Montréal, Québec?

. . . that there were over 300 Canadian athletes at the 1996 Olympics? There were more women than men.

Olympic history

The modern Olympics began in 1896 but the ancient Olympics started long before that. The ancient Olympics started in 776 BC. These games were in Greece. The first Olympic games lasted only one day and there was only one event—a race. The first athletes did not win a medal. They received a laurel wreath. No women were allowed at these games, not even to watch! The Roman emperor Theodosius stopped the ancient Olympics in AD 393.

Unit

1

And the winner is ...

Reach for the Star Pops!

Do you like contests? Do you often participate in them? Are you lucky? Find out what some other students think.

To understand what someone likes, dislikes, wants or prefers

1.2

● Read the comic strip.

● Write down what Sarah and Tommy like and dislike.

All about the contest

Sarah and Tommy have decided to enter the Star Pops contest. They find out more information about it.

- Work with your team. Listen to the conversation between Sarah and Tommy.

- Write down the information about the Star Pops contest on your contest card.

- Now choose the items and the container for your own contest.

HELP STATION

▶ **Numbers**

1	one	11	eleven	18	eighteen	60	sixty
2	two	12	twelve	19	nineteen	70	seventy
3	three	13	thirteen	20	twenty	80	eighty
4	four	14	fourteen	25	twenty-five	90	ninety
5	five	15	fifteen	30	thirty	100	one hundred
6	six	16	sixteen	40	forty	1000	one thousand
7	seven	17	seventeen	50	fifty	1 000 000	one million
8	eight
9	nine
10	ten

Sarah's great idea

How will Sarah and Tommy count the Star Pops? Sarah has a great idea.

● Read about Sarah's idea.

● Now choose the number of items for your team's contest.

To understand
what a person
or thing is

2.1

82

Double checking

Sarah and Tommy double-check the rules on the contest entry form.

Listen as Tommy reads the contest rules.

Look at the signs below.

Find the signs that match the contest rules. Write down the numbers.

1
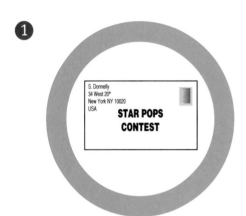

2

3

4
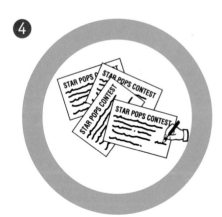

5

6

How to play

It's time to think of the instructions for your own contest.

- Work in your team. Think of three instructions to give your classmates.

- Write down the instructions.

Name of contest: **The Cotton Ball Contest**

Items: **cotton balls**

Container: **large plastic bag**

Instructions
1. Guess the number of cotton balls in the plastic bag.
2. Fill out the entry form.
3. Give your entries to Jacob.

Rules
1. You must be in grade five.
2. You may enter only once.
3. You may touch the bag but you must not open it.
4. You have to write your answer on the official entry form.

Prize: **a T-shirt**

Playing it right

Do you remember the rules for the Star Pops contest? Your contest needs rules too.

- Work with your team. Decide on the rules for your contest.

- Write them down.

- Explain the rules to your classmates.

And the winners are…

1. You will understand and give information about your personal experiences and the experiences of people close to you.

2. You will understand and give information about things outside your everyday life.

4. You will understand and give information about activities related primarily to school life.

It's time to participate in your classmates' contests. Who knows? This may be your lucky day!

- Make a poster to advertise your contest. On the poster, write:
  - the name of the contest
  - a drawing of the container and the items
  - the instructions
  - the rules
  - the prize.

- Participate in your classmates' contests. Good luck, and have fun!

Wow! That was fun!

What was your favourite contest?

I liked the balloon with the rice in it.

Me too. What an original idea!

The winners are Sarah and Tommy

The winners are . . . Sarah and Tommy! 53 347 Star Pops!!

Glossary

container: something that holds other items, like a box *(contenant)*
contest: game or competition *(concours)*
deadline: time limit *(date limite)*
entry form: official piece of paper used to enter a contest *(feuille d'inscription)*
to guess: to form an opinion without really knowing *(deviner)*
item: thing *(article)*
lucky: having good fortune *(chanceux)*
prize: award *(prix)*
to win: to be first in a competition *(gagner)*

Unit 10

THE SECRET ADMIRER

The secret admirer, Part 1

To understand the major elements of a story: characters, conflict, events

3.1

It's the day before Valentine's Day. Sonia is having a very exciting day at school. Find out what happens.

◉ Read the story.

◉ Answer these questions:
1. What happened to Sonia?
2. How many notes did she receive?
3. Where did she find the notes?

1. What a day! It all started in class that morning. Sonia sat down at her desk. She opened her pencil case and found a note. It was a love note! Sonia put it back in her pencil case.

2. During recess, Sonia put her hand in her coat pocket. She found another note. Sonia was getting curious!

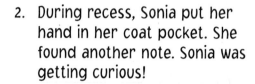

3. During math class, a paper plane landed on Sonia's desk. It was another note! "I have to find out who this is," Sonia thought.

4. That afternoon, Sonia opened her agenda to write down her homework. There was a note tucked inside. "I can't wait to get home," Sonia thought. "I want to know who my secret admirer is!"

The secret admirer, Part 2

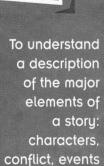

Sonia wants to know who her secret admirer is. She reads all her notes to try to find some clues.

🔊 Listen to the story.

🔊 Work with your team. Fill in the note cards.

🔊 Complete the storyline hearts.

To understand a description of the major elements of a story: characters, conflict, events

3.2

HELP STATION

▶ **Understanding stories**

WHERE = the place

WHEN = the time

WHO = the main characters

WHAT = the action

This is fun!

Sonia calls her friend Sayeeda to tell her about the notes.

🔊 Listen to the conversation between Sonia and Sayeeda.

🔊 Write down how Sonia feels and what she is going to do.

To understand
how someone
feels and what
someone is
going to do

1.5

I wonder who it is.

Sonia and Sayeeda are trying to figure out who the secret admirer is.

🔊 Listen to their conversation.

🔊 Circle the answers on your handout.

To understand someone's description of himself or herself

1.4

Billy   Lee   Igor   Jason   Pierre-Olivier   Martin   Colin

ACTIVITY 5

It's me!

You know who Sonia's secret admirer is. Now learn some new facts about your own teammates.

Play the Tell Me game with your teammates.

To describe yourself and other people

1.4

To use polite forms for saying thank you, sorry.

5.2

HELP STATION

► **Taking turns**

Keeping a secret

You're going to write a secret message to give to someone. Find out how to be a true secret admirer!

- Read the note from "M.T.".

- Listen to the cautions.

- Identify the information that does not follow the cautions.

Dear J.P.,
Happy Valentine's Day.
I think you are the best.
I have red hair and green eyes.
I love to play the piano.
I sit behind you in class.

Love, M.T.

Closure

Another secret admirer

1 You will understand and give information about your personal experiences and the experiences of people close to you.

4 You will understand and give information about activities related primarily to school life.

5 You will understand and use the common expressions people use when they speak and write to each other.

Now it is your turn to become a secret admirer. Make a Valentine heart puzzle to give to someone special.

- Write a special message on your Valentine heart.
- Cut the heart into puzzle pieces.
- Give the puzzle to a special person.

EXTRA! EXTRA!

Make an envelope for your puzzle. 1. Fold a sheet of paper in half. 	2. Fold over each side. 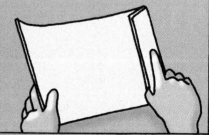	3. Tape or glue the sides. 
4. Insert your puzzle, fold over the top and seal it. 	5. Write the person's name on the front of the envelope and decorate it. 	

Glossary

fancy: decorated *(élaboré)*

to have a crush on: to be in love with *(aimer)*

heart: part of the body where feelings are imagined to arise *(coeur)*

hug: to hold someone close *(étreindre)*

lace: delicate fabric with holes that make a pattern *(dentelle)*

ribbon: long narrow strip of brightly coloured fabric used for decoration *(ruban)*

① Valentine cards

Long ago, most people couldn't read or write. They sang their Valentine messages to each other. Then people started to make their own cards.

About 200 years ago, Valentine cards were very fancy. They had real lace and ribbons. They often had hearts and cupids on them.

Now people send about 5 000 000 Valentine cards every year in Canada.

② Different ways to say "Be my Valentine"

Poetry

North, South,
East, West,
There's no question
You're the best!

Play on words

You're p-u-r-r-r-fect!
Be my Valentine!

Using symbols and pictures instead of words

My   longs 2 U.

③ On Valentine's Day, you could . . .

. . . play tic-tac-toe:

. . . say Happy Valentine's Day to five people who are not in your school or part of your family,

. . . do some Valentine math:

2 sweet
2 be
4 gotten

. . . find 14 words using the letters in V A L E N T I N E .

Unit 11

CHILDREN EVERYWHERE

Our world

ACTIVITY 1

To describe yourself and other people

1.4

Each country has a culture. All countries have special things. What do you know about different countries?

- Look at the map of the world.

- Describe the special things found in each country.

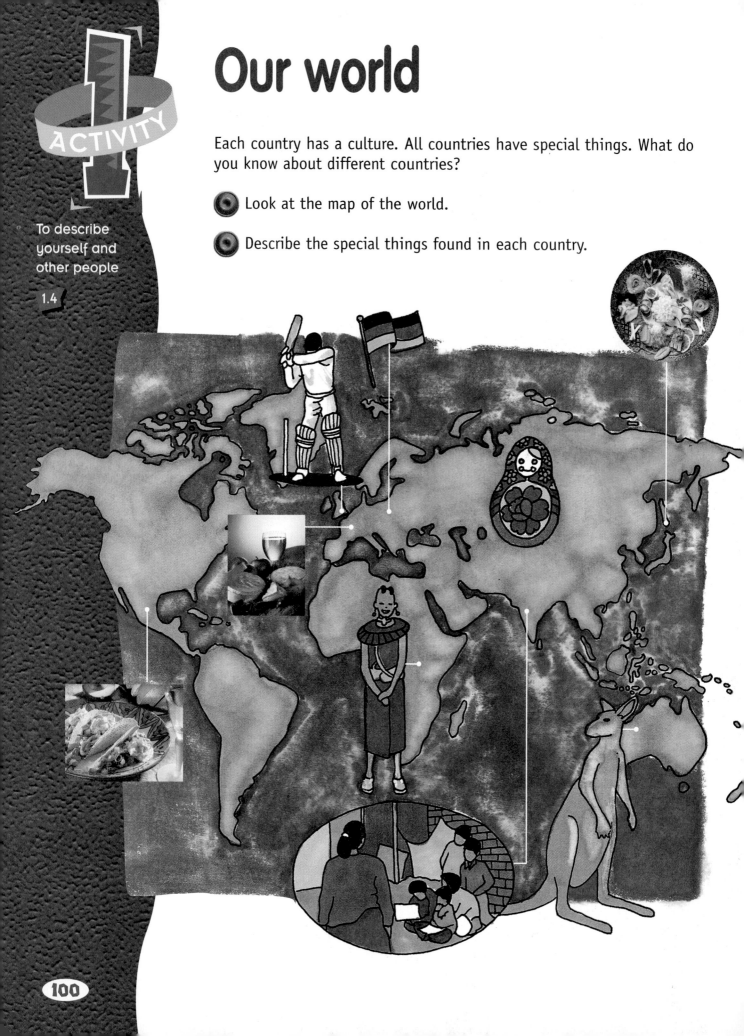

Around the world

Do you remember what you can find in different countries? What special things do you have in your own country?

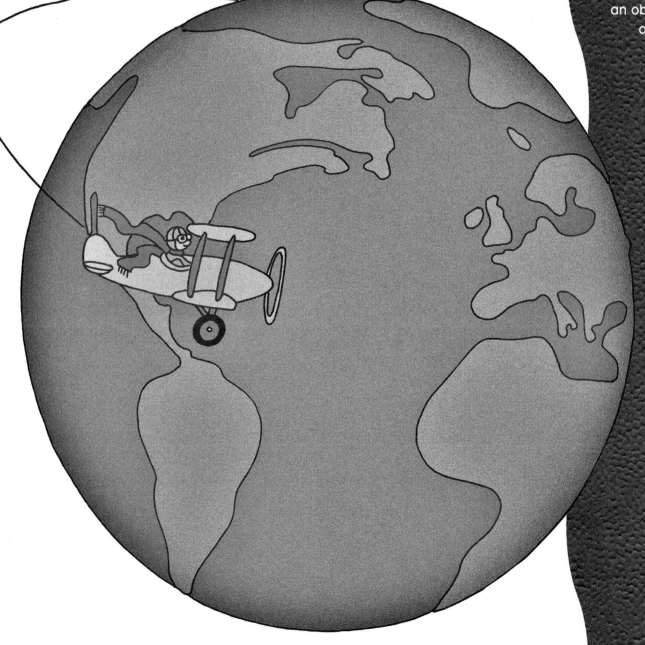

- Work with your team. Take turns reading the descriptions.

- Match the descriptions with the countries.

- Write down your team's answers.

Children, same and different

Do you know any children from other cultures? How are they different from you? How are they like you?

To understand what a person or thing is

2.1

Listen to the information about children of the world.

Write down how children are different and how they are alike.

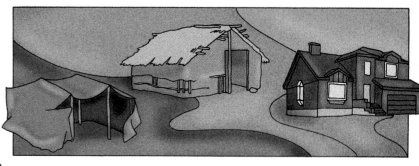

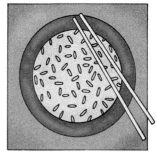

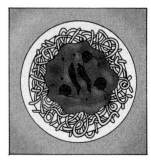

A day in the life

How do you spend your day? Do you think this is the same everywhere?

- Read the story about Meena and Libby.
- Write down how they are alike.
- Write down how they are different.

To understand
a comparison
between the
world of a story,
and yourself and
your own
experiences

3.3

A Day in the Life

This is how I spend my day.

I get up and wash myself. Then I get dressed.

Then I have breakfast.

After breakfast, I get my books. Then I'm on my way to school.

103

I like school.
I learn lots
of things.

After school,
I take care of
my pet.

I like to help
my mom
make the supper.

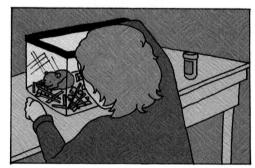

My brother and
I like to play
games before
we go to bed.

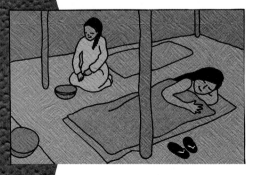

Soon, it's
"Goodnight".
I'm ready for another
day tomorrow.

What's for supper?

What sort of food do you eat at home? Children in different countries eat different food. Learn about the food that other children like to eat.

- Listen to the interview.

- Look at the pictures.

- Identify the food that each child likes to eat.

- Work with your team. Write an international menu.

HELP STATION

spaghetti

▶ **Food around the world**

bread

felafel

hamburger

pizza

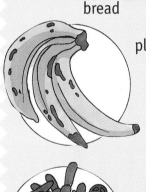

plantain

tacos

roast chicken

Closure

This is your life.

You have learned about life in other countries. But what about life here? Find out how your teammates live.

- Work with a partner.

- Ask your partner questions about his or her life.

- Tell your teammates about your partner.

HELP STATION

▶ **Asking for information and saying thank you**

Glossary

boiled: cooked in hot water *(bouilli)*

chick pea: type of pea *(pois chiche)*

country: nation *(pays)*

to cry: to weep *(pleurer)*

fried: cooked in hot fat *(frit)*

pancake: thin flat cake *(crêpe)*

rice: cereal grain *(riz)*

raw: not cooked *(cru)*

seafood: fish and shellfish *(fruits de mer)*

to shave: to remove hair with a razor *(se raser)*

to smile: to look happy *(sourir)*

to smile

rice and chick peas

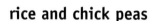

raw

Did you know . . . ?

In Russia, we eat pancakes with sour cream. They are called bliny.

In England, in most schools, we have to wear a school uniform.

In Bolivia, the most popular sport is soccer.

In Mongolia, some people live in a big, round tent. This is called a ger.

In Jordan, because it's so hot, we start school at 7 a.m. and finish at 12 noon.

Unit

12

CLEAN UP

Warm-up

To say how you feel and what you are going to do

1.5

What are some problems with our environment? How do we damage our planet? How do you feel about these problems?

⊙ Look at the picture.

⊙ Say how you feel when you see these problems.

HELP STATION

▶ **Expressing feelings**

I get angry when . . .   I don't like when . . .
I am happy when . . .   It hurts me when . . .
It makes me sad . . .   I get frustrated when . . .
I worry . . .   I feel . . .

KEEP
AREA
CLEAN

Please be careful.

Help everyone keep the environment clean.

Work with your team. Make a poster for your neighbourhood.

To give a
warning or
caution

4.5

The clean-up contest

Why not enter the neighbourhood clean-up contest? Find out what you must do.

- Listen to the ad on the school radio.

- Find out what you must do to enter the contest.

- Write the answers on your information card.

What can we do?

Vanessa, Keero, Aaron and Pilar are talking about the clean-up contest.
Find out what they are going to do.

⊙ Read the story.

⊙ On your handout, check what Vanessa and her friends can do.

Right. Do you have any ideas? What can we do for the contest?

Well, I can write a story.

Great. Aaron, what about you?

Um. I don't know.

Can you make a poster?

No, I can't draw very well. I know, I can collect cans and bottles. I can take them to the recycling bin.

Good. Pilar, what can you do?

O.K. I can help you. I can make a list of all the problems I see.

I can do a neighbourhood survey. You know, find out what our neighbours are doing to help the environment.

Yeah, then we can tell our neighbours.

All right. Everybody ready? Let's clean up!

113

To understand
how to get to a
certain place

4.3

To understand
polite forms for
saying thank
you, sorry.

5.2

Collection route

Aaron has organized a bottle- and can-collection day. He will explain the route that the group will follow.

 Listen to Aaron's directions.

Follow the collection route on your map.

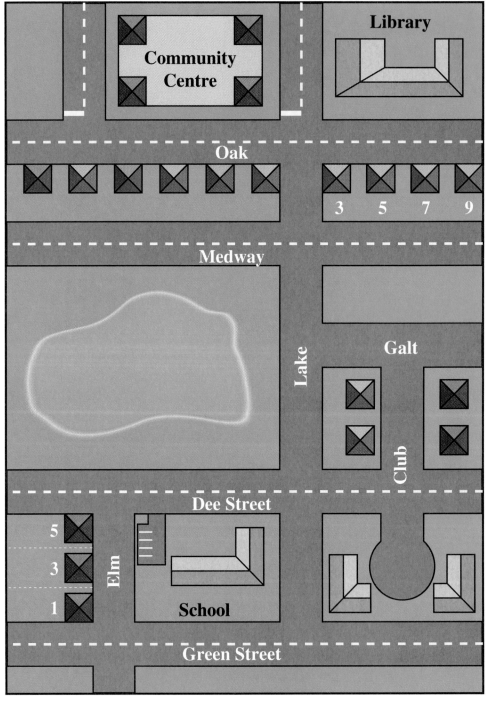

The adventures of a candy wrapper

Vanessa has written a story for her contest entry.

 Read Vanessa's story.

 Work with your team. Place the story cards in order.

I was in my usual place, on the shelf in the store. I watched the people go by. "I hope somebody buys me today," I thought.

Just then, a boy came in. He walked towards me. I was excited. He picked me up, paid for me and walked out of the store.

He unwrapped the chocolate and started to eat. He threw me on the ground. "Oh no," I thought. "Where will I go now?"

Suddenly, the wind swept me up. I flew through beautiful gardens in a nice, clean neighbourhood. "Oh, I hope I don't land here," I thought. "The gardens are so clean. Why didn't he just put me in the garbage can? It's much better for the environment, and for me!"

Up, up and away. I flew around. Then the wind stopped. I slowly floated to the ground. I landed on the street in the clean neighbourhood. "Oh dear," I thought. "I should not be here."

I heard voices. "Hey Jacques, look. Somebody threw garbage on the ground," a girl said. "It makes me angry. Remember what we learned in school yesterday? We have to keep our neighbourhood clean."

The boy turned around. It was the boy who bought me. He looked ashamed. He picked me up. "You're right, Josée," he said. "We all have to do our part. Starting today, I'm going to be careful."

Jacques walked to the garbage can. He put me in. Finally, I felt better. I think Jacques learned an important lesson.

Closure

Ready, steady, clean up!

Part A

What can you do to clean up your neighbourhood? It's time for you to create your team clean-up project.

⦿ Write down your ideas.

⦿ Complete your team project plan.

⦿ Ask your teacher to check your plan.

Part B

⦿ Now put your project together.

⦿ Present your clean-up project to the rest of the class.

Glossary

ashamed: feeling bad about doing something wrong *(honteux)*

aware: conscious *(conscient)*

candy wrapper: paper covering a candy/chocolate bar *(papier d'emballage)*

entry: project for a contest *(inscription)*

garbage can: container for garbage *(poubelle)*

neighbourhood: area where people live *(quartier)*

participant: person who takes part in a contest *(participant)*

survey: questions asked to different people *(sondage)*

worried: concerned *(inquiet)*

worried

candy wrapper

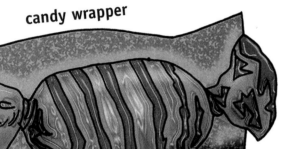

neighbourhood

garbage can

Reduce, reuse, recycle

1. If we recycle 75% of the paper we use, we can save about 35 million trees per year.

2. Recycle newspapers and paper.

3. Write on both sides of your paper.

4. Reuse old wrapping paper to wrap new gifts.

5. Use a cotton lunch bag or a lunch box instead of paper bags.

6. Recycle cans and bottles.

7. Always put garbage in the garbage can.

8. Turn off the light when you leave a room.

9. Turn off the tap when you are brushing your teeth.

10. Walk or bike short distances. Try not to take the car.

Every effort counts. We can all do something to help our planet.

Do you care about planet Earth?

Take the test to see if you are doing things to help our environment.

Read each statement and choose your answer.

	Always	Sometimes	Never
I use a lunch box/cotton lunch bag.	■	■	■
I recycle newspapers and paper.	■	■	■
I write on both sides of my paper.	■	■	■
I reuse wrapping paper.	■	■	■
I recycle cans and bottles.	■	■	■
I turn off the light when I leave a room.	■	■	■
I turn off the tap when I'm brushing my teeth.			

Points

Give yourself: 2 for always
                 1 for sometimes
                 0 for never

12 - 14 points: Great! You're doing well. Keep it up!
 8 - 11 points: Not bad! You're almost there!
 0 - 7 points: Uh-oh! Try to do more for our planet.

Unit 13

The Tin Box

How it all started

The adventure started when Ms Whitaker asked Nina and Gage to clean out her garage.

🔘 Listen to the telephone conversation between Gage and Ms Whitaker.

🔘 Find out when and where the story takes place.

🔘 Fill in the story keys with this information.

To understand a description of the major elements of a story: characters, conflict, events

3.2

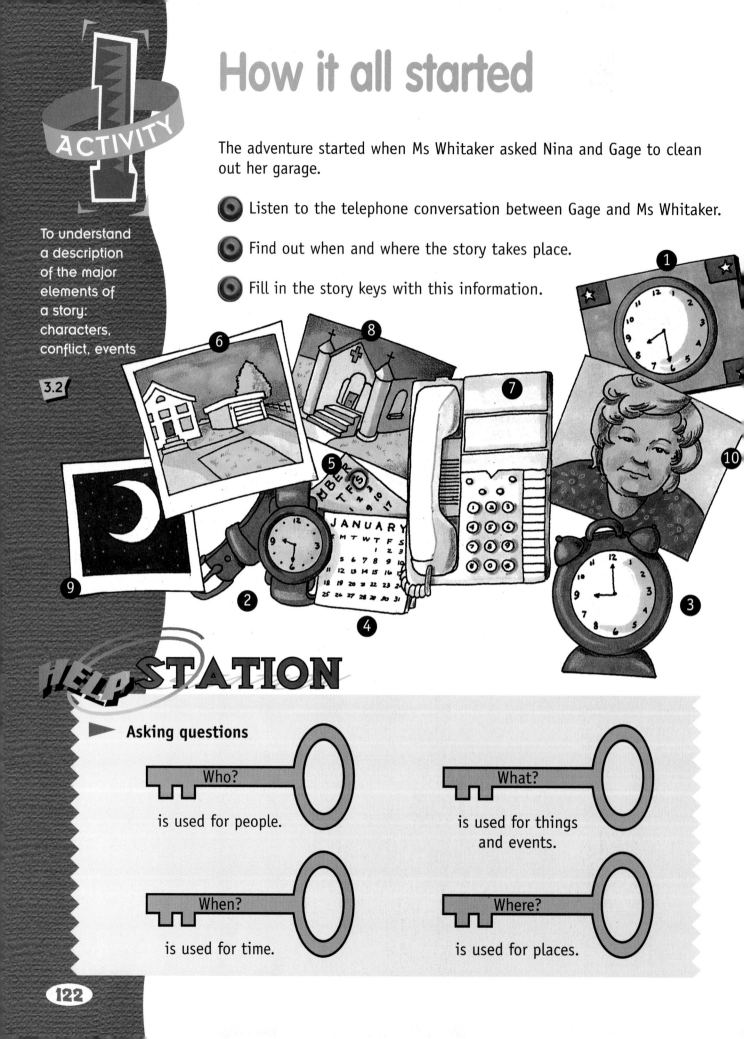

HELP STATION

▶ **Asking questions**

Who? is used for people.

What? is used for things and events.

When? is used for time.

Where? is used for places.

Should we or shouldn't we?

Nina and Gage go to clean out Ms Whitaker's garage. They discover a tin box. They can't decide what to do.

- Listen to the first part of the story.
- Find out what Nina and Gage think.
- Add new information to your story keys.

To understand a report about a person, an animal, an event, an object or a place

2.3

① It's not ours.

BOING!

② It's not locked.

③ Why don't we ask Ms Whitaker first?

④ No one will know.

SWISH SWISH

⑤ It doesn't belong to us.

⑥ It looks private.

I don't think we should.

Come on, let's do it!

⑦ She told us to throw out the garbage.

123

A. Look! It's a map.

Nina and Gage finally decide to open the tin box.

🔊 Listen to more of the story.

🔊 Add new information to your story keys.

To understand a description of the major elements of a story: characters, conflict, events

3.2

B. Buried treasure

Where does the map lead? Is there buried treasure?

🔘 Listen to the directions.

🔘 Follow the directions on your map.

Can you find it?

It's your turn for a treasure hunt. Try to find your classmates' buried treasure. Happy hunting!

To tell someone how to get to a certain place

⦿ Make a treasure hunt for your classmates. Your teacher will tell you what to do.

⦿ Try to find the buried treasure in your classroom.

4.3

HELP STATION

► **Giving directions**

Turn left.

Turn right.

Go straight ahead.

Go around.

Go under.

Go over.

She's behind . . .

He's next to . . .

The message

Gage and Nina follow the map. They arrive at a big old oak tree. They are very excited. The treasure is not far now!

🔊 Read the end of the story.

🔊 Add new information to your story keys.

🔊 Try to decipher the coded message.

To understand a description of the major elements of a story: characters, conflict, events

3.2

To understand a factual description of a person, an animal, an event, an object or a place

2.2

Yuk! It's dirty and wet and deep. Let's use a stick.

Good idea.

I can't. My hand's too big. Come on.

Go on! Put your hand in the hole.

You do it.

Feel anything?

Not yet. Oh yes! There's a paper or something, but I can't get it. You'll have to stick your arm in there.

Are you sure there are no snakes or squirrels or rats?

That's it? A piece of paper?

VEXMR SC BOKNI.
IYE NOCOBFO SD.
WC GRSDKUOB.

It's a secret message. Help me break the code.

Oh, I've got it. You replace one letter with another. The fourth word is "you" and O = E.

127

Tell us what happened.

Now you have finished the story, play the question card game.

 Add new information to your story keys.

 Play the question card game.

To describe the major elements of a story: characters, conflict, events

3.2

What I think

ACTIVITY

To say whether
you like a story
and what you
feel about it

3.4

How do you feel about the story? Did you like it?

Write down your opinion of the story. Look at the help station for some ideas.

▶ **Useful adjectives**

boring *(ennuyeux)*	dull *(ennuyeux)*	fantastic *(fantastique)*
challenging *(stimulant)*	easy *(facile)*	fun *(amusant)*
difficult *(difficile)*	exciting *(passionant)*	interesting *(interessant)*

I think it's a great story. I was anxious to find out what happened.

Me too!

I don't think it's very realistic. I guess it was O.K.

Me too!

I liked the coded message.

Me too!

Closure
The tin box

It's time for you to make a class collage about the story "The Tin Box".

◉ Work with your team. Complete your story keys.

◉ Make a collage to represent your section.

◉ Add your section to the class collage.

"It's a secret message."

"8:30 Saturday morning."

"It's a tin box."

"Come on. Let's get the treasure."

Glossary

to be against something: to disagree with *(contre)*

bird bath: container of water in which birds clean themselves *(bain pour les oiseaux)*

to break a code: to find the solution for a code *(déchiffrer)*

buried: covered *(enterré)*

to deserve: to earn *(mériter)*

to be for something: to agree with *(pour)*

locked: closed with a key *(fermé à clef)*

oak: type of tree *(chêne)*

pine: type of tree *(pin)*

tin: soft silver-coloured metal *(étain)*

treasure hunt: search for treasure *(chasse au trésor)*

oak

bird bath

buried

to break a code

locked

tin

Break the code!

There are lots of different codes. The code in Nina's message is called a substitution code. You replace each letter with another letter.

Here is another message for you to decipher.

S DRSXU MYNOC
KBO PKXDKCDSM!
VOD'C GBSDO XYDOC
SX MYNO DY YEB
PBSOXNC.

A = K; B = L . . .

I THINK CODES ARE FANTASTIC! LET'S WRITE NOTES IN CODE TO OUR FRIENDS.

Unit

14

FUND FIESTA

Money fun

ACTIVITY 1

To say what
a person,
an animal,
an event,
an object or
a place is

2.1

Sometimes groups need to collect money for special activities. There are many ways to raise this money.

Name the things you can do to raise money. Look at the picture for some ideas.

PLAY-A-THON

Super Garage Sale!

Fund fiesta

The Mossley School Band needs money for a special activity. Find out what they do.

- Listen to the story "Fund Fiesta".

- Follow the pictures in your book as you listen.

- Play the story cube game with your teammates.

CAR WASH
$145

DONATIONS
$74.50

COOKIES
AND JUICE
$163

GAMES
$132

PLAYED
$82

Cash tips

Now you know how the band raised their money. Here are some other suggestions to raise money.

🔘 Listen to the students' conversation.

🔘 On your handout, colour in the activities they suggest.

What can you do?

What could you do to raise money for a special activity?

🔘 Work with your team. Suggest ways that you can raise some money.

🔘 Write down your ideas on your team handout.

ACTIVITY

To ask
someone to
do something
or to go
somewhere

4.6

Playing it safe

It's good to have fun when you do your fund-raising project. But it's also very important to be careful and to work safely.

- Listen to the safety tips.
- Write down the Dos and Don'ts to make sure your project is safe.

To understand a warning or caution

4.5

When you need help

You might need help for your fund-raising project. Ask your teacher or another adult.

- Read the expressions in the help station.
- Use them to ask for help whenever you need it.

To ask someone to help you

4.2

HELP STATION

To use polite forms for saying thank you, sorry

5.2

▶ **Asking for help**

Being polite

Could you help me?
Excuse me.
I need help to . . .
Please could you . . .?
I'm not sure how to . . .

Thanks a lot.
Do you think you could help me?
Thank you very much.
How do I . . .?
Sorry to bother you.

Closure

Our fund-raising project

2 You will understand and give information about things outside your everyday life.

4 You will understand and give information about activities related primarily to school life.

You'll need to advertise your fund-raising projects in your neighbourhood. Here's what to do.

⦿ Work with your team. Say what you can do to raise money for your activity.

⦿ Design a pamphlet to advertise your activity.

⦿ Present your pamphlet to the class.

Glossary

bottle drive: collecting bottles to exchange for money *(collecte de bouteilles)*

fund raiser: project used to collect money *(levée de fonds)*

greeting card: card given for special occasion *(carte de souhaits)*

housework: work around the house *(ménage)*

music camp: camp for musicians *(camp de musique)*

raffle: lottery *(loterie)*

saxophone

trombone

clarinet

trumpet

flute

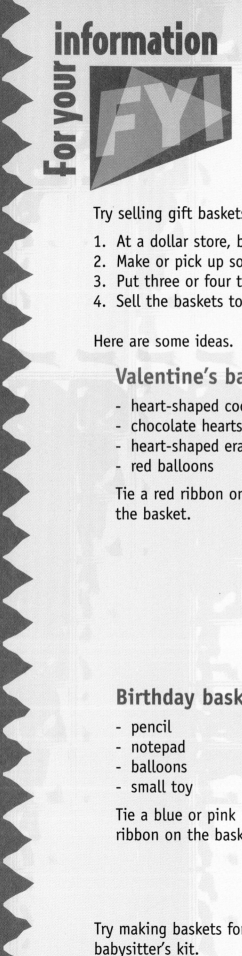

information

FYI

For your

Gift baskets

Try selling gift baskets for special occasions.

1. At a dollar store, buy some small baskets.
2. Make or pick up some treats to include in your baskets.
3. Put three or four things in each basket.
4. Sell the baskets to your family, neighbours and friends.

Here are some ideas.

Valentine's basket

- heart-shaped cookies
- chocolate hearts
- heart-shaped eraser
- red balloons

Tie a red ribbon on the basket.

Easter basket

- chocolate eggs
- a small stuffed animal
- Easter stickers

Tie a yellow ribbon on the basket.

Birthday basket

- pencil
- notepad
- balloons
- small toy

Tie a blue or pink ribbon on the basket.

Try making baskets for other occasions—Christmas, anniversaries, Halloween, babysitter's kit.

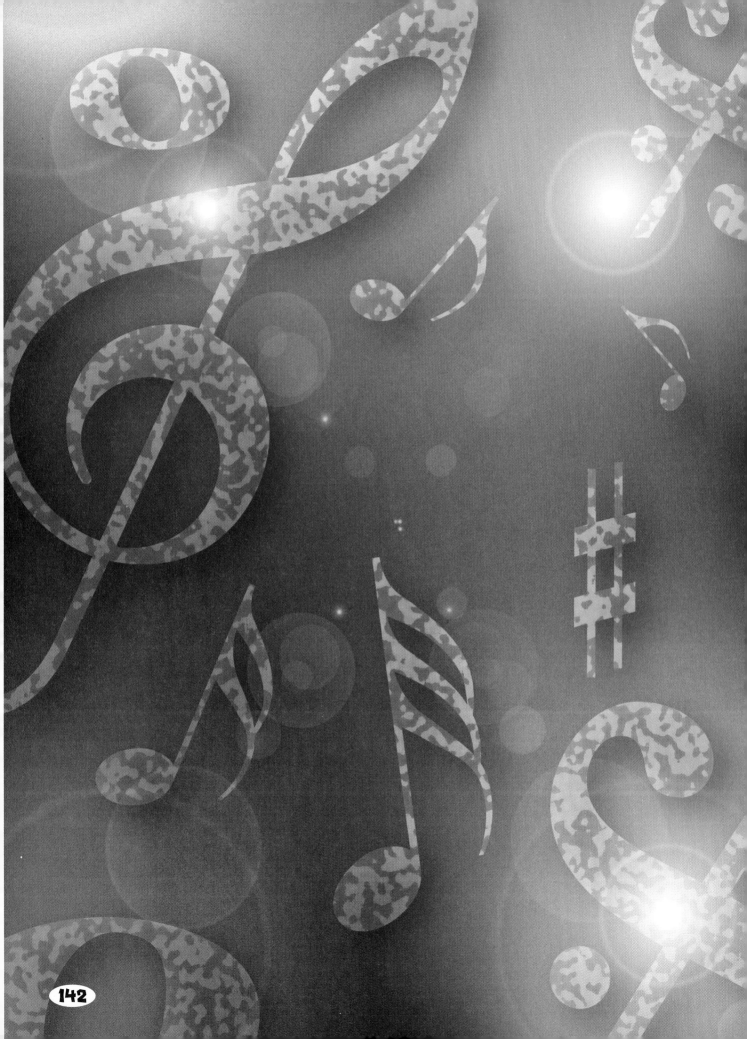

Families

We're going to talk about our families
I want to know about your family
I'll tell you who's in my family
Then you'll tell me about yours
Children have different families
So talk to me about your family
Who wants to start talking about them?
Be the first to tell me of yours

There are three with my mother
There's me and my big brother
We live together in an apartment
Right downtown on the second floor
We're not rich but we're happy
We get along in our small family
Life's O.K. for mom, me and my brother
It's your turn—tell me of yours

Well I lost my first family
They died when I was little
I've been adopted by two people
Who give me love and a lot more
It's so nice to live together
And I hope it lasts forever
I'm so happy with my new family
Who could ask for anything more?

As long as you have love within the family
Warm hearts within the family
Good feelings within the family
Great fun within the family
Have faith in your family
Put trust in your family
Be patient with your family
And you'll have love and a lot more

Team Up!

Team up, look great great great
Team up and co-operate
Team up, have a lot of fun
Team Up! makes you number one

One gets the handouts, Two speaks out here
Three is the captain, so make a cheer
Four's the recorder, who takes notes down
We depend on each other, round and round

We are a good team, we have fun
We work real hard to get our work done
I depend on you, you depend on me
We pull together, we don't disagree

Teacher, give us our work, we have the sprit now
Our team has a cheer, it's wow,wow,wow
We co-operate, know what to do
So watch us go—we're in the same canoe!

Where Are the Animals?

Where are the animals? Show me the animals.
Where are the animals? Show me where they are.

It's big, it's white, it's dangerous
It walks on four big feet
It runs, it swims, it plays around
Lives in the Arctic and eats meat

It's the biggest creature that swims in the sea
When it comes up, it's easy to see
It's grey, it's dark, it's long and wide
It's a big, big mammal, not easy to hide

It's fast, it's quick, it's small, it's light
Looks like a dog, goes out at night
It's red, it's brown, it's sometimes white
It likes to play in the moonlight

These are two cousins. They live in the woods
One's brown, one's grey—they both look good
They walk, they run and get around
With their four quick hoofs barely touching
the ground

Christmas

Bells will ring all day for it's the holidays
Joy will follow you wherever you go
Yes, it's Christmas time Santa's here today
To bring some joy and make it snow

One thing worries me when it's the holidays
Do the children of the world feel like I do?
Are they happy and joyful?
Will they get gifts today?
Santa make sure that they're O.K.

So, giddy-up Santa can't you see
I've been so good, look at me
All year round, yes I've been good
Bring me presents if you could

When it's Christmas time and we're on holiday
It's time to play, do something new
Peace and joy warms hearts in the holidays
So open yours, do what I do

How I love the warm feeling of holidays
People smile, wave to you and say hello
Stars shine bright for you on Christmas holidays
So wear a smile and make it glow

Spot Dance

Do it and you'll be hot hot hot
Follow me on the spot spot spot
Let's dance, now make it hot hot hot
Follow me on your spot spot spot

Raise your hands in the air, swing them all around
Take one step to the front and stomp on the ground
Turn to the left, turn to the right, now look straight ahead
Take one step back this is what I said, I said

Now bend down, touch the floor, then jump real high
Look to the left, look to the right, reach to touch the sky
Point to the front, point to the back, now point ahead
O.K. lend me your ears, listen to what I said, I said

Take one step to the side, swing all around
Now step back to your spot and make a big sound
Go ahead then go back, go to your place
This spot dance is out in space. So . . .

Feel the Magic

When you're shy, you're sometimes lonely
When you're happy, you're never blue
When you are with other people
You have them and they have you.

When you smile at other people
They look back and smile at you
Warm warm hearts are never broken
Feel the magic inside of you.

Don't be shy, be open-hearted
Let the people look inside of you
They need love from other people
'Cause they feel just like you do.

Song 7

Change the World

Do you want to change the world, change the world?
Save the world from pollution
Do you want to clean it out, be a good scout
Save the world from pollution

Do you want to help me out, to change the world
And free the world from pollution
Do you want to feel O.K., do what you may
To free the world from pollution

It has been many generations
That the world has turned round and round
But not many years that we find pollution on the ground
So, let's get together, to make it
Healthy, clean and sound

This great world is yours and mine
Let's clean up our playground

Reference section

1. CLASSROOM LANGUAGE

Read   Write   Listen   Speak

Quiet, please.   Can you help me, please?   Please speak English.

I don't understand.   Yes, I understand.   Listen, please!

I've finished.

Open your book to page 34.

Close your books.

Good morning.

Good afternoon.

Good evening.

Good night.

Good work, everybody.

See you tomorrow.

2. DIRECTIONS

Turn right.

Turn left.

Go straight ahead.

north, south, west, east

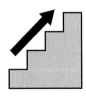

up

down

in front of

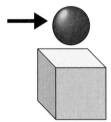

back

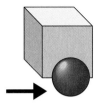

above/over

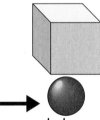

below

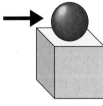

on top of

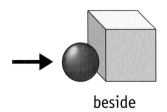

beside

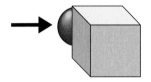

behind

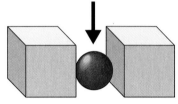

between

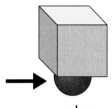

under

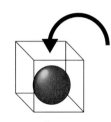

in

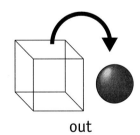

out

angry *(fâché)*

bored *(ennuyé)*

excited *(excité)*

happy *(content)*

lonely *(seul)*

nervous *(nerveux)*

sad *(triste)*

shy *(timide)*

worried *(inquiet)*

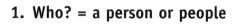

4. QUESTION WORDS

1. Who? = a person or people

Who is your teacher this year?

Ms Baxter.

2. What? = a thing or things

What's your favourite wild animal?

A beaver.

3. When? = a time

When are you going to Toronto?

When is the party?

In July.

At half past seven.

4. Where? = a place

Where do you live?

In Sillery.

5. Why? = reason

6. How? = manner

7a. How many? = quantity

7b. How much? = quantity

8. Which? = choice

157

5. NUMBERS

1 one	**11** eleven
2 two	**12** twelve
3 three	**13** thirteen
4 four	**14** fourteen
B five	**15** fifteen
6 six	**16** sixteen
7 seven	**17** seventeen
8 eight	**18** eighteen
9 nine	**19** nineteen
10 ten	**20** twenty

21 twenty-one
22 twenty-two
23 twenty-three
24 twenty-four
25 twenty-five
26 twenty-six
27 twenty-seven
28 twenty-eight
29 twenty-nine
30 thirty

40 forty
50 fifty
60 sixty
70 seventy
80 eighty
90 ninety

100 one hundred
1000 one thousand
100 000 one hundred thousand
1 000 000 one million

JANUARY 1999
nineteen ninety-nine

1st first	**2nd** second	**3rd** third	**4th** fourth	**5th** fifth	**6th** sixth
7th seventh	**8th** eighth	**9th** ninth	**10th** tenth	**11th** eleventh	**12th** twelfth	**13th** thirteenth
14th fourteenth	**15th** fifteenth	**16th** sixteenth	**17th** seventeenth	**18th** eighteenth	**19th** nineteenth	**20th** twentieth
21st twenty-first	**22nd** twenty-second	**23rd** twenty-third	**24th** twenty-fourth	**25th** twenty-fifth	**26th** twenty-sixth	**27th** twenty-seventh
28th twenty-eighth	**29th** twenty-ninth	**30th** thirtieth	**31st** thirty-first			

Special events

HAPPY HALLOWEEN!

MERRY CHRISTMAS

HAPPY EASTER

HAPPY ST PATRICK'S DAY!

HAPPY MOTHER'S DAY

HAPPY FATHER'S DAY

HAPPY BIRTHDAY

HAPPY VALENTINE'S DAY

Encouragement	Congratulations	Travel	Apology
Get well soon	Well done	Bon voyage	I'm sorry
I'm sorry	Way to go!	I miss you	Please forgive me
Better luck next time		Welcome back	
Don't give up	**Thanks**		**Hello**
Cheer up		**Love**	
You can do it	Thank you		Just to say "hi"
	Thanks so much	I love you	
Luck		Love you lots	
Good luck			
Break a leg!			

Size

tall   medium   short   big   thin

Hair

curly   wavy   straight

Eyes

brown   blue   green   hazel

short   medium   long

Face

round   square   oval   long

black   brown   red   blond

I have long black hair and black eyes. My face is round. I am not very tall. I wear glasses.

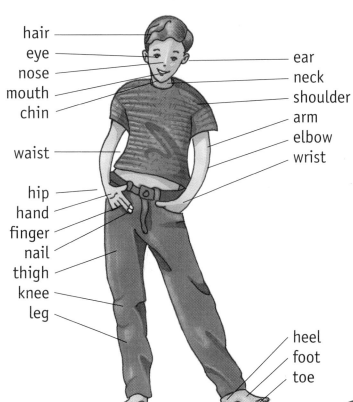

hair
eye
nose
mouth
chin

ear
neck
shoulder
arm
elbow
wrist

waist

hip
hand
finger
nail
thigh
knee
leg

heel
foot
toe

161